Also by David Miller

Reassembling Still: Collected Poems, Shearsman Books, 2014

Spiritual Letters, Contraband Books, 2017

Towards a Menagerie, Chax Press, 2019

Matrix I, Guillemot Press, 2020

Matrix II, Guillemot Press, 2020

CIRCLE SQUARE TRIANGLE
fragments of an autobiography

David Miller

Spuyten Duyvil
New York City

Excerpts from this work have appeared in the following online and print journals: *Long Poem Magazine, otata's bookshelf, STRIDE* and *Tears in the Fence*.

for Dodo, with love

Part One

Part One

1

I was passing by the old house
& my mother came out & saw me

"it's you isn't it?" she said
"you can't come in she wouldn't let you

she hates you"
yes my sister hated me

& my mother was dead

elongated
preternaturally tall & thin

but her face
was her face

**

a neighbour's son
broke his legs diving

while
a former school friend

racing a motorcar
crashed

& then died
in a coma

one I didn't like
he tore the feathers

off live birds

the other I did
these my contemporaries

O yes amongst others
I hated & those I loved

did I hate?
perhaps

dislike
distrust

disapproval
at any rate

**

hated? I

hated how
people behaved

& also what
they believed

sometimes &
sometimes it seemed

impossible & sometimes
again

possible

in the straits

**

sinews & wire
wire could just be wire? no

through & past & back

through the brakes
& bulrushes

a mask I wore
(it was wartime)

cornbrakes

cinematic
(dream)

bunting
flapping

in wind
**

2

"what doesn't further love's cause
is loveless

& at best a hindrance"

ah but I telephoned
& telephoned

& telephoned
from stations stations

near parks
& from the house

& it all it all it all
was broadsided

or hit by
a sidewinder or

imploded & ex-

**

cigarette in her mouth
as she searched amongst books

for me I mean for what
I'd asked

– someone tipped wine
onto his head

from an upstairs window
he was a poet

of course

**

strayings...

for life... be life be alive

& death beckons

**

I died
for love

& yet here
you are

trains cars taxis
motorbikes buses

let's say a Russian
death

but for now
thrown out of every

watering hole
in the city

& even
elsewhere

**

let's say
a chance meeting

between a straw bonnet
& a jar of pickles

on a mortuary slab?

or with a carving knife
thrown in?

— "has anyone said
you're Pre-Raphaelite?" I asked

thinking of Lizzie Siddal
in Rossetti's paintings

"oh everyone says that"

– I didn't have a straw bonnet
nor a jar of pickles

nor a carving knife

& certainly not
a mortuary slab

not even
a hospital bed

**

"don't pray for the animals
ask that they should be able

to pray for us"

after I'd gone to a meeting
to pray for animals

yes

I stood on the parapet
afterwards

afterwards
looking out over the city

a mild evening but some wind
a bereaved woman

& I so hopeless
to say anything

**

trying to get home
through seemingly

endless streets
& drunken crowds

so late
transport's stopped

yet research libraries
still open

& you could unlock
odd doors

leading to towers
with bibliographers

& also toilets
for those caught

in the night

**

strange meals
pasta & salad

for instance

why strange?
incongruous

I was leaving

**

3

no liking
or sadness

certainly

for the skinheads
who pummelled

& kicked me
& a friend

out of pure spite

"oh the poor young men"
so a benighted neighbour

"what terrible backgrounds
they must have"

no sorrow for them
no sorrow for her

miserable
misplaced

& mindless
sympathy I

would spew
you out

I remember
yes ribs kicked

& glasses
scooped up

afterwards

**

in Singapore
in a Hindu temple

a shenai player
& a hand drummer

so good my jaw
dropped

& pimps & prostitutes
outside the door

of my hotel

**

table tennis
on the ship

& I reading
W S Graham

& then later
in London

Graham
so drunk

I was embarrassed
silly young man

sought him later
in Madron

without luck

but Cornsh folk
said

when I was writing a postcard
"say they need to send you money"

I was longhaired sure

**

Notting Hill a
prostitute

my neighbour yes
my neighbour? yes

came to the door
late at night

so drunk
her daughter later

scaffolding as
art

"please play with me"
the daughter ah no

impossible
as

**

did anyone say
chronology?

that it featured?

my downstairs
neighbours

dead & their flat
demolished

making way
for the young rich

**

so drunk
as to fall down

collapse
in the doorway

4

"a basket
in the water"

(& I
not)

**

religious
edu-

cat-
ion

& strappings
& slaps

to the head

(bulrushes
& water)

5

a dance or at least
jazz & my older female friend took me there

music playing & older girls dancing

"boy" a girl said earlier
much earlier an older girl

"would you like a jam doughnut?"

how delicious what she didn't want
sprinkled with icing sugar

**

the hotel
in central London

I've stayed in
so often

it doesn't exist

**

basil
on the window sill

**

a fledgling
sea gull

out on the grass
all afternoon

& even evening
in heavy rain

in the same spot
in our garden

tried feeding it
tried lead-

ing it
to

somewhere out
of the rain

to no avail

& another I saw
in the alcove

of a shop front
in central Bridport

ah equally
so lost

**

we fed the fledgling
sardines mackerel & bread

I even stroked its feathers
that first night

so cold & wet

& now it's flown

**

dragonflies
& red admirals

& cabbage whites
& green

woodpeckers

– but what were the books
I consulted

& what were the meals
we had?

I & those
others

**

circle square triangle
"is there nothing else?

perhaps nothing"

or
rectangle

triangle
circle

overlapped tri-
angle

& circle

I ground my own ink
from ink sticks

but my friend
the collagist

stuck paper down

after words

**

a blue circle
to what

avail?

clouds scudding
waters bloodied

trees scudding
in ink

& wine
in exile

& I?

Part Two

Part Two

1.

she had her granddaughter
with her when she called

at my sister's home
"I'm your brother's friend" she said

– birds fly & land here
spaceships will for my sister

& take her far away
when all else is destroyed

vindication yes
or spectral

delusion

**

at my mother's
memorial

service

at a local
Lutheran

church

poet friends
attended &

one read

musician friends
played

 – & now a poet
tells me

to buy & prepare
lunch

for a visiting
poet

(American)

& everyone has a grant
while I

pay my own fees
at this dream

university

**

late
lunar

neighbourhood

– harm
was done

daughter
against mother

through torment

**

mirror
or glass

an agony
either

way
a

statistic
yes a box

to be ticked yes

while torment
rages

& harm's
irrevocably

done

**

death

2.

no decoration
no

elaboration
no

**

persuasion &
power

or

the language
of poverty

renunciation
all

I never

agreed to nor aspired
to

never a slave
never a master

**

goodbye

3.

the school
for non-violence

had long since gone

idols?
images?

I
wanted

to speak

**

it was London
in the early 70s

I met painters
I met poets

how lost I was
& how lost

I continued

& now? I
address

& redress

how many failings
how much to be redressed

dressed
undressed

– *look*
into

your own
human

& sometimes
merciless

eyes

to learn
charity

**

& poverty's scarcely
a virtue for the poor

where wealth rules?

scarcely

rule &
non-rule

virtue
is

opposed to power?

poor
virtue?

poverty
where power

rules

**

easy for the rich
or the comfortable

you could say
to admire the poor

understandable
also

for the poor
to admire the rich

& the comfortable
or

sometimes
at least envy

in either case
when it suits them

or is this
cynical? I ask

the poor have less
& more to lose

but I ask the dead
with temerity

& with trembling

I ask
the dead

**

circle square triangle

could
it be

square circle triangle?
triangle square circle?

circle square triangle
yes

**

lipped

to what

lips?

given (1) the circle
(2) the square

(3) the triangle

she kissed
her kist

I wrote
in my teens

to be
re-

minded

Part Three

1.

the mirror blank
in a gallery so

rich I wondered why
I was there

reflection
image

occluded
obscured by clouds

as
sky by clouds

am I there?
I

must write this
with my life's blood?

no not clouded

the mirror's
blank

the divine
page

2.

you made the film
my dear friend

& sent it to me

I watched it
& watched it

the old house
the neighbourhood

the streets
the houses

ordo amoris

I watched it
& watched it

& now I cannot

**

the first tear
the second tear

the third tear

the

sheet
tears

tears
& then

dissolves

**

cir-
cles

inter-
linked

an
end-

ing

**

hedgehog
mouse

sparrow
pigeon

dunnock
starling

or
I must decide

which books to take
& how to shower

& even piss

in this
univers-

ity

that at night
I must attend

& travel
by bus

to get there

**

the earth
the ground

**

& what
might succeed us?

us?
(a different

us)
or

other
animals?

hedgehogs
dwindling

here in Bridport

starlings
seldom seen

except
at West Bay

**

different? perhaps
but do we really

become better? not
I'd say

on the whole – try
as some do

someone's sister may be mad
but also vicious

& her spaceships
 – rescuing

from this doomed world

would accept her
though she's cruel to old women & dumb creatures

& unrepentant

3

Basil Bunting's old home
could have been mine

Ric Caddel's
recommendation

– poets

Northumberland not
where I ended up

oh I did need a home
& the offer was there

no job though
no money

& I couldn't

but London?
dream

in
dream

the streets

art galleries
temples

& recital halls

& no job
no money

**

even though
Bunting's home

was on a new suburban
housing estate

(I've since heard)

where he felt isolated
 – *slave barracks* he wrote

at least no blood
from sacrifices

spattered on market food
nothing

but boiled wheat
with sugar

to eat

**

a red towel
& yes a ring

blackbirds splashing
 – frenetic

in the birdbath
in the rain

pampas grass
high & luxuriant

waving
in wind & rain

**

rain continuing
late into night

rooftops

doors
stairs

& rooms
I've lived in

shall I again?
no

except
for this

this
in sleep

this
folly

of return

where rooms
open to keys

are now occupied
by others

**

never
prepared

nor
unprepared

yet married
& it's autumn

brushes held & deployed
ink & water

cascades

or a mural I'd painted
above a friend's bed

– Melbourne

wash basins with soap
three

& a spray of water

water's
flow

hands &
eyes & nose & lips & chin

stutter
of sight

red towel
& ring

Part Four

Part Four

sun's circle's
cut

& it dies
in darkening

& dark waters
fishing

a theophany
a hierophany

a necrology

**

memory
surely

serves well

or serves ill
ah no argument there

home or position

no place
for poetics

let alone poetry

when rape murder
beatings

hold sway

& yet there must be

**

a bruise
a blurred

circle

sparks spat out
grinding of metal

pouring of molten metal

...& so dies
in darkening

or dark waters

*weep no more
sad fountains*

(sung)

**

brussels sprouts
planted in ground

(where else?)
now snow

& eaten by deer

the sun dies

**

waiting for the old rice
to boil

the birds
might like it

when cooled down

but in fact
unimpressed

– was he derailed?
no

he became famous
within his circle

was he derailed?
yes

a circle
within

a derailed
circle

**

you can only deny
the divine

through language
& image-making

created to address
the divine

the discourse
contaminated

& uplifted

the language
& the image-making

ultimately

can shed little
even nothing

however stripped
& stultifying

& simplistic
some try

to render them

**

a sister's madness

a circle
cut

shadows
shadows

shadows

nights working
at the Source

a bookshop
where I stayed

all night

reading Bunting &
Raworth & Jones

& Harwood
&

ah scarcely selling anything

**

could I win the round
without throwing a single punch?

could I refuse
the fight? rhetoric's

gone to ground (I wish)
& I

lived in the Hudson house

while writing my thesis
of course it didn't

work out
loud Spanish music

from the floor below

& my clarinet stolen
& I

attacked
for being in someone's path

a kicking

bruises
recorded

**

debased language
& image-making

not to be minimised

bloated verbiage
or one-dimensional

triumphs of word
& image

writers & artists
lost in labyrinthine irony

or swallowed up
by rhetoric

all of this
to be countered

contraflow

**

I did live there
in Ladbroke Grove

without benefit
of anything much

to the yew it was given
its rich dark mantle

of undying foliage

to keep guard over the bodies
& souls

I was there to write
& I wrote

W H Hudson...
the colour of bracken

living or dead
we cover our dead

with earth
& with green

& flowering plant

**

my mother's
sewing machines

her sewing room
& my sister

**

however likeable
the performer

her performance
was poor

& my Australian friend
recalled someone back home

I hadn't seen or heard from

the garden of...
the garden

of....

**

it bounds
it encloses

it points upwards

I can intend
only

thus

& disclose
as it falls

Part Five

Part Five

a bull caught
in a thicket

a sun
sliced to death

**

or eclipsed
or

gone
down

to death

**

a statue
or

an image
inscribed

in stone
or made

in a mosaic

but a field mouse
stares me down

when caught
late at night

in the kitchen

& Bunting
lies dead

as Jones or Graham
even Raworth & Harwood

& Turnbull

I wish
we could talk

once
or once more

but of what indeed? indeed
nothing

crosses my dumb lips
or my mute mind

**

I'd come from Australia
& thought I'd

do what the English had done
& I didn't even

start

everything botched
botched from the beginning

**

my dear woman friend
I did love

her friendship I
betrayed

& her husband's
friendship

O also

cigarette in mouth
she searched

amongst books
for me

an old story

**

yes an old story
old because it

comes back &
comes back

& I want respite

**

demolished?

eviscerated
at any rate

**

& the door
had caved in

or been broken down
more likely the latter

& there I lived

or reduced to sleeping
on a balcony

the bed set up there
in everyone's view

& I moved
(cleft)

to a place
chosen

**

bracelet
dropped

in snow
drifts

**

brussels sprouts
in the snow

**

strange archives
I've been to

in strange
old buildings

eccentric artists
yet respected

whose holdings
I've sorted out

& been pleased to

**

& I saw you
my beloved

my wife

in or near these places
where art galleries

museums
were abundant

slums also

industrial slums

**

skewed
syntax

struck

by astonishment
or loss

or hopelessness

**

an
in-

sect

(fire-
fly)

danc-
ing

(....)

or a girl
at night

alone
in a

laundrette

listening
& dancing

to a
radio

**

*I could see
your shadow*

*but I couldn't
see you*

pharmacies
& stationers

cafeterias

churches

& museums also

despite the snow

**

rampant he spoke:
"if there is a Satan

you should abjure him"

but he wasn't a lion
just a mouse

pretending to be a lion
pretending? no

standing in? perhaps

askew

**

hamstrung

I still
however

will witness
will tell

Notes

These few notes are purely for acknowledgement and/or to help avoid confusion.

Part 3:1
"I must write this with my life's blood": paraphrase of Max Scheler, from the essay '*Ordo Amoris*', in his *Selected Philosophical Essays*, tr David R Lachterman, Northwesttern University Press, 1973

Part 3:3
"slave barracks": Basil Bunting, quoted in Richard Burton, *A Strong Song Tows Us: The Life of Basil Bunting*, Infinite Ideas, 2013

Part 4
"weep no more, sad fountains": John Dowland
Section beginning "I did live there": italicised phrases are from W H Hudson, all of them quoted in my book *W H Hudson and the Elusive Paradise*, Macmillan, 1990

DAVID MILLER was born in Melbourne, Australia, but has lived in the UK for many years. His recent publications include *Black, Grey and White: A Book of Visual Sonnets* (Veer Books, 2011), *Reassembling Still: Collected Poems* (Shearsman, 2014), *Spiritual Letters* (Contraband Books, 2017), *Towards a Menagerie* (Chax Press, 2019), *Matrix I & II* (Guillemot Press, 2020), *Vitruvian Shadows* (The Red Ceilings Press, 2020) and *Some Other Days and Nights* (above/ground press, 2021). He has compiled *British Poetry Magazines 1914-2000: A History and Bibliography of 'Little Magazines'* (with Richard Price, The British Library / Oak Knoll Press, 2006) and edited *The Lariat and Other Writings* by Jaime de Angulo (Counterpoint, 2009) and *The Alchemist's Mind: a book of narrative prose by poets* (Reality Street, 2012). He is also a musician and a member of the Frog Peak Music collective., and has performed and recorded as part of The Mind Shop and with Louise Landes Levi, Ken White, Rod Boucher and others. Previous books and chapbooks have appeared from Enitharmon, Gaberbocchus, Arc, Stride, Reality Street, Burning Deck, Singing Horse, Chax, hawkhaven and Harbor Mountain.